JESUS LOVES YOU

Contact Us:

✉ MyBibleWorkbooks@gmail.com

📷 Projectkingdomcome

f Projectkingdomcome

PROJECT KINGDOM COME
ISBN 978-1-961786-16-5

Get The Entire
Workbook Series!

THE BOOK OF
GENESIS
BIBLE-BASED WORKBOOK

...male and female He created them. Genesis 1:27

Take an adventure into the amazing Book of Genesis
and test your knowledge as you go!

PROJECT KINGDOM COME

THE BOOKS OF
EXODUS & JOSHUA
BIBLE-BASED WORKBOOK

See, afraid stiff. Joshua 10:12

Take an adventure into the amazing Books of Exodus and Joshua
and test your knowledge as you go!

PROJECT KINGDOM COME

THE BOOKS OF
I & II SAMUEL
BIBLE-BASED WORKBOOK

And they anointed David king over the house of Judah. 2nd Samuel 2:4

Take an adventure into the amazing Books of 1st and 2nd Samuel
and test your knowledge as you go!

PROJECT KINGDOM COME

THE BOOKS OF
I & II KINGS
BIBLE-BASED WORKBOOK

and he shall come and sit on my throne and be king. 1st Kings 1:35

Take an adventure into the amazing Books of 1st and 2nd Kings
and test your knowledge as you go!

PROJECT KINGDOM COME

THE BOOKS OF
ESTHER & RUTH
BIBLE-BASED WORKBOOK

And she obtained grace and favor in his sight. Esther 2:17

Take an adventure into the amazing Books of Esther and Ruth
and test your knowledge as you go!

PROJECT KINGDOM COME

THE BOOKS OF
DANIEL & JOB
BIBLE-BASED WORKBOOK

they brought Daniel and threw him into the lions' den. Daniel 6:16

Take an adventure into the amazing Books of Daniel and Job
and test your knowledge as you go!

PROJECT KINGDOM COME

THE BOOK OF
MATTHEW
BIBLE-BASED WORKBOOK

Behold a virgin shall be with child. Matthew 1:23

Take an adventure into the amazing Book of Matthew
and test your knowledge as you go!

PROJECT KINGDOM COME

THE BOOK OF
MARK
BIBLE-BASED WORKBOOK

Let us go into the next towns, that I may preach there also. Mark 4:38

Take an adventure into the amazing Book of Mark
and test your knowledge as you go!

PROJECT KINGDOM COME

THE BOOK OF
LUKE
BIBLE-BASED WORKBOOK

...there they crucified Him. Luke 23:33

Take an adventure into the amazing Book of Luke
and test your knowledge as you go!

PROJECT KINGDOM COME

THE BOOK OF
JOHN
BIBLE-BASED WORKBOOK

...I am the resurrection and the life. John 11:25

Take an adventure into the amazing Book of John
and test your knowledge as you go!

PROJECT KINGDOM COME

THE BOOK OF
ACTS
BIBLE-BASED WORKBOOK

...In the name of Jesus Christ of Nazareth, rise up and walk. Acts 3:6

Take an adventure into the amazing Book of Acts
and test your knowledge as you go!

PROJECT KINGDOM COME

THE BOOK OF
REVELATION
BIBLE-BASED WORKBOOK

Look, He is coming with the clouds, and every eye will see Him. Revelation 1:7

Take an adventure into the amazing Book of Revelation
and test your knowledge as you go!

PROJECT KINGDOM COME

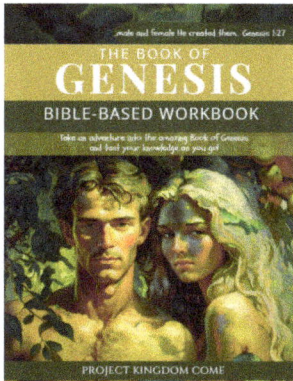

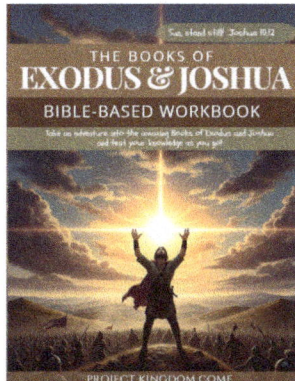

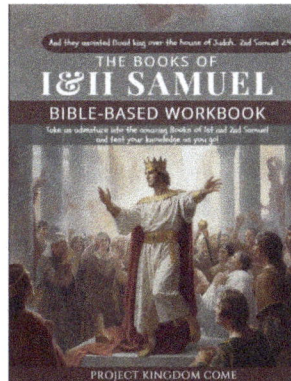

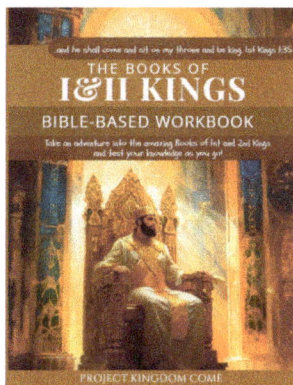

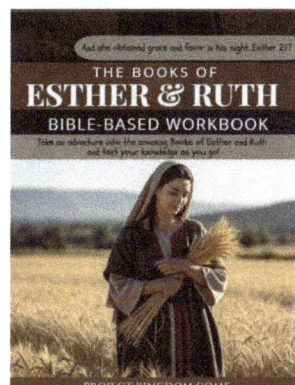

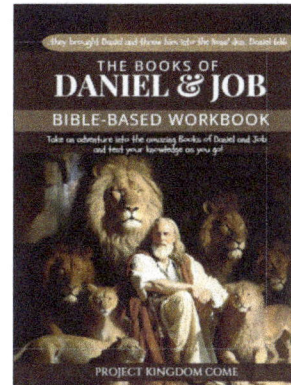

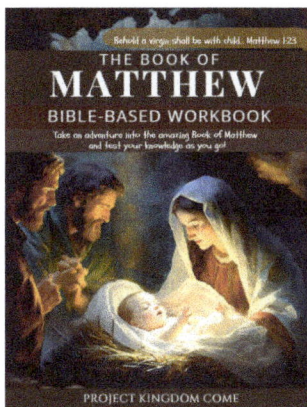

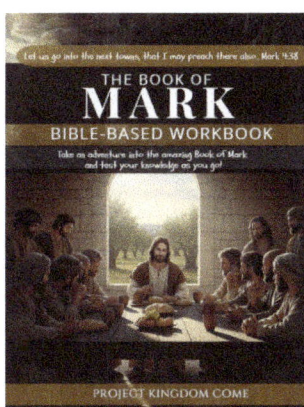

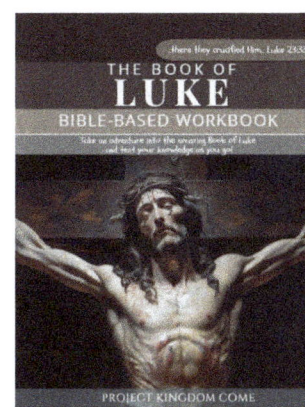

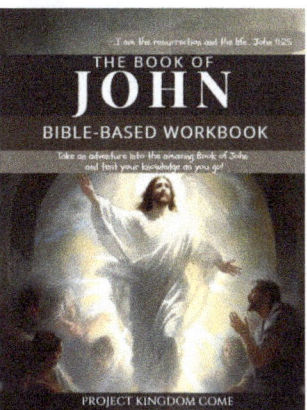

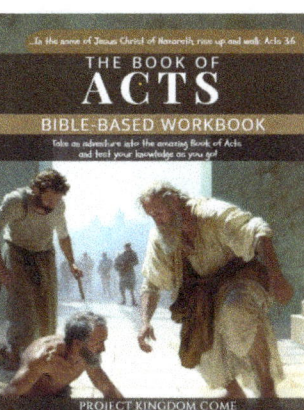

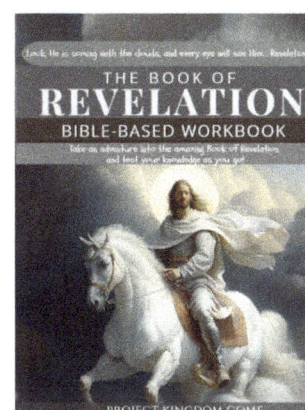

WWW.MYBIBLEWORKBOOKS.COM

PROJECT KINGDOM COME

This workbook belongs to:

_____

_____

_____

Leave your mark!

HOW TO USE THIS WORKBOOK

This workbook is designed to help young people explore the treasures in God's Word while having fun, growing in faith, and learning how to search the Scriptures for life's answers.

Here is what you will find inside:

Multiple Choice Questions

Each question comes directly from Scripture and includes a reference verse to help with locating the answer in the Bible. If possible, use a physical Bible to search for the answers.

Weekly Segments

Questions are grouped in weekly categories that could also be completed in a shorter or longer time frame.

Weekly Memory Verses

At the start of every week is a Bible verse to memorize. Each day of that week will repeat that memory verse with a chance to test memorization at the end of the week.

Certificate of Completion

At the end of the workbook, please find a Certificate of Achievement, ready for the child's name and parent or teacher's signature. Celebrate the accomplishment of studying an entire book in the Bible!

Answer Key

The workbook contains an answer key to serve as a support tool for parents or teachers reviewing the responses.

Recommendation for Parents and/or Teachers: Review the responses with your child or student and discuss lessons learned or interesting insights, to improve the child's retention and enrichment in the knowledge of God's word.

You can do all things through Christ who gives you strength!
Philippians 4:13

SAMPLE QUESTION...
HOW TO USE THIS WORKBOOK

Reading the reference verse will always lead you to the correct answer!

In the beginning, God created: (Genesis 1:1)

(A) The Heavens and the Earth
B. Heaven and Earth
C. Heaven only
D. Earth only

The number that comes after the book is the 'Chapter'

This is the name of a book in the Bible

Joshua 1:8

The number after the chapter is the 'Verse'

NOW TEST YOURSELF! FIND JOSHUA CHAPTER 1 VERSE 8 IN YOUR BIBLE!

INTRODUCTION: THE BOOK OF DANIEL

Faith in the Fire. Vision in the Darkness. God in Control.

The Book of **Daniel** is a powerful story of **faithfulness, wisdom, and divine protection**. Even in a land far from home, Daniel stood strong in his faith and never bowed down to the culture around him. He was taken into captivity, given a new name, and surrounded by kings who worshiped idols, but Daniel never forgot who he was or who his God is.

God gave Daniel **wisdom beyond his years**, courage to stand alone, and visions that revealed kingdoms yet to come. Whether facing the fiery furnace, a den of lions, or the pressure to compromise, Daniel remained faithful — and God always came through.

As you read Daniel, you will discover:

- **God honors those who stand for truth**
- **God gives wisdom to those who seek Him**
- **Even in exile, God is in control**
- **God reveals mysteries to the faithful**
- **Our obedience opens the door to supernatural protection**

This book is more than history, it is a call to be unshakable in your faith, even when everyone else is bowing. You will meet friends who walked through fire and came out without a burn, and a man whose prayers moved heaven and shut the mouths of lions.

You're not just reading Daniel's story, you're stepping into your own. Be bold. Be faithful. Be fearless. The same God who walked with Daniel walks with you!

"But the people who know their God shall be strong, and carry out great exploits."
Daniel 11:32b

WEEK 1

> 1. Which King of Babylon came to Jerusalem and besieged (captured) it? (Daniel 1:1)
>
> A. King Cephas
> B. King Nebuchadnezzar
> C. King Jehoiakim
> D. King Cyrus

> 2. What kind of young men did the chief eunuch look for (Daniel 1:4)
>
> A. Good looking, gifted, intelligent
> B. Strong and muscular
> C. Obedient
> D. Prayerful

WEEK 1 MEMORY VERSE: DANIEL 2:22

He reveals deep and secret things; He knows what is in the darkness, and light dwells with Him.

WEEK 1

> 3. How long were the young men to be trained before serving the King? (Daniel 1:5)
>
> A. One full year
> B. Three (3) years
> C. Four (4) years
> D. Seven (7) years

> 4. What were the names of the young men chosen to be trained in order to serve the King? (Daniel 1:6)
>
> A. Shadrach, Meshach, and Abednego
> B. Daniel, Hananiah, Mishael, and Azariah
> C. Daniel, Mishael, and two others
> D. Four young men from Judah

WEEK 1 MEMORY VERSE: DANIEL 2:22

He reveals deep and secret things; He knows what is in the darkness, and light dwells with Him.

WEEK 1

5. **What new names did the chief eunuch give the young men? (Daniel 1:7)**

A. Belteshazzar, Shadrach, Meshach, and Abednego
B. Daniel, Hananiah, Mishael, Azariah
C. The young men asked the chief eunuch not to change their names
D. The young men were given new names by the King himself

6. **Why didn't Daniel want the King's food and wine? (Daniel 1:8)**

A. It had been offered to idols and would defile him
B. Daniel was not used to royal food
C. The King's food was too fancy for Daniel
D. Daniel wanted to go on a diet

WEEK 1 MEMORY VERSE: DANIEL 2:22

He reveals deep and secret things; He knows what is in the darkness, and light dwells with Him.

WEEK 1

> **7. What food was Daniel given instead of the King's food and wine? (Daniel 1:12)**
>
> A. Vegetables and water
> B. Food from the temple
> C. Bread and fruit
> D. Food that honored God

> **8. What special ability did God give to Daniel? (Daniel 1:17)**
>
> A. Understanding visions and interpreting dreams
> B. Preaching with boldness
> C. Leading worship
> D. Healing the sick

WEEK 1 MEMORY VERSE: DANIEL 2:22

He reveals deep and secret things; He knows what is in the darkness, and light dwells with Him.

WEEK 1

9. Why was the King pleased with Daniel and his friends? (Daniel 1:19-20)

A. They were respectful to the King's servant
B. They were the most hardworking in the group
C. They were ten times wiser than all the magicians and astrologers
D. They never complained during training

10. What did the King ask his magicians and enchanters to do about his dream? (Daniel 2:1-5)

A. Tell him what the dream meant
B. Help him remember why he was feeling anxious
C. Tell him the dream and its meaning
D. Comfort him until he felt better

WEEK 1 MEMORY VERSE: DANIEL 2:22

He reveals deep and secret things; He knows what is in the darkness, and light dwells with Him.

WEEK 1

11. What was the punishment for not telling the King his dream and its meaning?
(Daniel 2:5)

A. They would be sent away in shame
B. They would be torn limb from limb and their houses destroyed
C. They would be put in the fiery furnace
D. They would be thrown into the lions' den

12. What reward did the King promise for revealing the dream and its meaning?
(Daniel 2:6)

A. A royal banquet
B. Gifts, rewards, and great honor
C. A high position in the palace
D. A robe of many colors

WEEK 1 MEMORY VERSE: DANIEL 2:22

He reveals deep and secret things; He knows what is in the darkness, and light dwells with Him.

13. What did Daniel do after learning of the King's plan to destroy all the wise men? (Daniel 2:16-18)

A. He asked the King for more time
B. He prayed by himself
C. He asked his friends to seek God with him
D. All of the above

14. What happened after Daniel and his friends sought God for the interpretation? (Daniel 2:19)

A. God showed Daniel the mystery in a vision at night
B. They all received the answer at the same time
C. They fasted and waited seven days
D. Daniel had a dream about a statue

WEEK 1 MEMORY VERSE: DANIEL 2:22

He reveals deep and secret things; He knows what is in the darkness, and light dwells with Him.

KEEP GOING, YOU'RE DOING GREAT!

> The Lord gives me wisdom.
> From His mouth I receive knowledge and understanding.
> (Proverbs 2:6)

Great job completing the week!

Did you memorize the daily verse?
Test yourself by writing it here...

_____

_____

_____

_____

_____

Use this space to draw a scene from the Bible or reflect on something you learned, felt or experienced...

15. **What did Daniel do after God revealed the mystery to him? (Daniel 2:19-24)**

A. He blessed the God of heaven and praised Him
B. He told his friends what God had shown him
C. He asked Arioch to take him to the King
D. Both A and C

16. **When the King asked Daniel to tell him the dream and its meaning, what did Daniel say? (Daniel 2:27-30)**

A. "No wise man, enchanter, magician, or diviner can explain the mystery, but God in heaven can reveal it."
B. "God revealed this mystery so you, O king, may understand your thoughts."
C. "This mystery was not revealed to me because I have greater wisdom than other men."
D. All the above

WEEK 2 MEMORY VERSE: ROMANS 12:2

And do not be conformed to this world, but be transformed by the renewing of your mind, that you may prove what is that good and acceptable and perfect will of God.

WEEK 2

17. What did the head of gold in the dream represent? (Daniel 2:36-38)

A. Wealth and power
B. The king of the Jews
C. King Nebuchadnezzar and his kingdom
D. The glory of earthly rulers

18. What does the Rock cut from the mountain without hands represent? (Daniel 2:44-45)

A. The return of King Nebuchadnezzar
B. The Kingdom of God that will never be destroyed
C. A mysterious kingdom in the future
D. The Second Coming of Jesus Christ

WEEK 2 MEMORY VERSE: ROMANS 12:2

And do not be conformed to this world, but be transformed by the renewing of your mind, that you may prove what is that good and acceptable and perfect will of God.

<<<<< >>>>>

19. What did King Nebuchadnezzar say after Daniel interpreted his dream?
(Daniel 2:46-47)

A. He became afraid of Daniel
B. He said Daniel's God is the God of gods and the revealer of secrets
C. He gave the glory to himself
D. Both A and C

20. How did the King reward Daniel after he interpreted the dream? (Daniel 2:48-49)

A. He gave him many great gifts
B. He made him ruler over Babylon and chief of the wise men
C. Daniel asked the King to appoint his friends to positions of authority
D. All the above

WEEK 2 MEMORY VERSE: ROMANS 12:2

And do not be conformed to this world, but be transformed by the renewing of your mind, that you may prove what is that good and acceptable and perfect will of God.

WEEK 2

<<<<< >>>>>

21. What did the King command people to do when the golden image was set up? (Daniel 3:1-5)

A. Bow down and worship it
B. Worship after hearing music
C. Offer personal prayers to their god
D. Both A and B

22. What was the punishment for not worshiping the golden image? (Daniel 3:6)

A. They would be thrown into the fiery furnace
B. They would be thrown into the lions' den
C. They would be killed by hanging
D. They would be beaten with whips

WEEK 2 MEMORY VERSE: ROMANS 12:2

And do not be conformed to this world, but be transformed by the renewing of your mind, that you may prove what is that good and acceptable and perfect will of God.

WEEK 2

<<<<< >>>>>

> ### 23. Who refused to worship the golden image? (Daniel 3:12)
>
> a) Daniel & Hananiah
> b) Daniel, Shadrach, Meshach & Abednego
> c) Shadrach, Meshach & Abednego
> d) Daniel only

> ### 24. What did the young men say when they were brought before the King? (Daniel 3:13-18)
>
> A. "We don't need to answer you"
> B. "Our God can save us"
> C. "Even if He doesn't, we won't bow"
> D. All the above

WEEK 2 MEMORY VERSE: ROMANS 12:2

And do not be conformed to this world, but be transformed by the renewing of your mind, that you may prove what is that good and acceptable and perfect will of God.

WEEK 2

<<<<< >>>>>

> **25. What happened when the young men were thrown into the furnace?** (Daniel 3:24-27)
>
> A. A fourth man appeared
> B. They were not harmed
> C. Their clothes smelled like fire
> D. Both A and B

> **26. Who did the King say was the fourth man in the fire?** (Daniel 3:25)
>
> A. It was Daniel
> B. It was an angel
> C. He looked like the Son of God
> D. He was one of the soldiers

WEEK 2 MEMORY VERSE: ROMANS 12:2

And do not be conformed to this world, but be transformed by the renewing of your mind, that you may prove what is that good and acceptable and perfect will of God.

WEEK 2

<<<<<<   >>>>>

"

27. Why did King Nebuchadnezzar command that no one speak against the God of Shadrach, Meshach, and Abednego? (Daniel 3:29)

A. He was amazed at how God saved them
B. He wanted everyone to like them
C. He planned to make them rulers
D. He started to believe in many gods

"

28. What did the tree in the King's dream represent? (Daniel 4:20-22)

A. A proud person
B. King Nebuchadnezzar's power and greatness
C. Mount Sinai
D. A forest that reached heaven

WEEK 2 MEMORY VERSE: ROMANS 12:2

And do not be conformed to this world, but be transformed by the renewing of your mind, that you may prove what is that good and acceptable and perfect will of God.

Your word I have hidden
in my heart, that I might
not sin against You
(Psalm 119:11)

Great job completing the week!

Did you memorize the daily verse?
Test yourself by writing it here...

_____

_____

_____

_____

_____

Use this space to draw a scene from the Bible or reflect
on something you learned, felt or experienced...

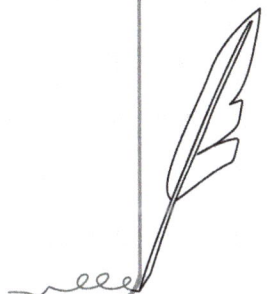

<<<<< **WEEK 3** >>>>>

29. What did the dream mean when the King's mind was changed to that of a beast? (Daniel 4:25)

A. He would live with wild animals
B. He would be eaten by lions
C. He would become ruler of the animal kingdom
D. He would turn into a lion

30. What advice did Daniel give the King after interpreting the second dream? (Daniel 4:27)

A. Repent and do what is right
B. Be kind to the poor
C. Stay silent and hope nothing happens
D. Both A and B

WEEK 3 MEMORY VERSE: DANIEL 11:32B
But the people who know their God shall be strong, and carry out great exploits.

31. How long did it take before King Nebuchadnezzar lost his kingdom after Daniel warned him? (Daniel 4:29-33)

A. 10 years

B. 7 years

C. 3 years

D. 12 months

32. How long was King Nebuchadnezzar to live like a wild animal? (Daniel 4:32)

A. 10 years

B. 7 periods of time

C. 3 years

D. 1 year

WEEK 3 MEMORY VERSE: DANIEL 11:32B

But the people who know their God shall be strong, and carry out great exploits.

33. What did King Belshazzar and his guests do at the feast? (Daniel 5:1-4)

A. Used the holy cups from God's temple
B. Praised false gods made of gold and silver
C. Celebrated a royal wedding
D. Both A and B

34. What happened after they drank from the temple items? (Daniel 5:5-9)

A. A hand appeared and wrote on the wall
B. The King was terrified
C. His wise men could not explain the writing
D. All of the above

WEEK 3 MEMORY VERSE: DANIEL 11:32B

But the people who know their God shall be strong, and carry out great exploits.

WEEK 3

<<<<< >>>>>

"

35. What did the Queen suggest when no one could read the writing on the wall?
(Daniel 5:10-12)

A. Call for Daniel
B. Call for the young Hebrew men
C. Call the soldiers
D. Call for Daniel's family

"

36. What did the Queen say about Daniel?
(Daniel 5:10-12)

A. He had the spirit of the gods
B. He had wisdom and understanding
C. He could solve hard problems
D. All the above

WEEK 3 MEMORY VERSE: DANIEL 11:32B
But the people who know their God shall be strong, and carry out great exploits.

37. What reward did King Belshazzar offer Daniel if he could read the writing? (Daniel 5:16)

A. He would be the third ruler in the kingdom
B. He would be clothed in a purple robe & gold chain
C. A royal crown
D. Both A and B

38. What did Daniel say about King Nebuchadnezzar? (Daniel 5:18-21)

A. God made him powerful
B. He became proud and lost his mind
C. He lived like an animal
D. All the above

WEEK 3 MEMORY VERSE: DANIEL 11:32B

But the people who know their God shall be strong, and carry out great exploits.

WEEK 3

39. What was King Belshazzar's sin? (Daniel 5:22-23)

A. He didn't humble himself
B. He drank from God's holy cups
C. He praised idols instead of God
D. All the above

40. What does "Mene" mean in the writing on the wall? (Daniel 5:25-26)

A. Your kingdom has ended
B. You have been weighed and found lacking
C. Your kingdom will be divided
D. God has numbered your kingdom and finished it

WEEK 3 MEMORY VERSE: DANIEL 11:32B
But the people who know their God shall be strong, and carry out great exploits.

WEEK 3 <<<<< >>>>>

> **41. What does "Tekel" mean in the writing on the wall? (Daniel 5:25-27)**
>
> A. You have been weighed in the balance and found wanting
> B. Your kingdom has ended
> C. Your kingdom will be divided
> D. God has taken your life

> **42. What does "Peres" (Parsin) mean? (Daniel 5:25-28)**
>
> A. You've been found guilty
> B. Your kingdom will be split and given away
> C. God has judged your family
> D. You will lose your crown

WEEK 3 MEMORY VERSE: DANIEL 11:32B

But the people who know their God shall be strong, and carry out great exploits.

I can do all things through Christ
who strengthens me
(Philippians 4:13)

Great job completing the week!

Did you memorize the daily verse?
Test yourself by writing it here...

_____

_____

_____

_____

_____

_____

Use this space to draw a scene from the Bible or reflect on something you learned, felt or experienced...

43. **What happened after Daniel interpreted the writing on the wall? (Daniel 5:29-30)**

A. The King was angry and punished Daniel
B. Daniel was honored with royal gifts
C. The King was killed that same night
D. Both B and C

44. **How many satraps did King Darius appoint to rule the kingdom? (Daniel 6:1)**

A. 12
B. 120
C. 24
D. 70

WEEK 4 MEMORY VERSE: PSALM 18:2
The LORD is my rock and my fortress and my deliverer; My God, my strength, in whom I will trust; My shield and the horn of my salvation, my stronghold.

<<<<< # WEEK 4 >>>>>

45. What made Daniel stand out among the officials? (Daniel 6:3)

A. He always told the truth
B. He was very nice to everyone
C. An excellent spirit was in him
D. He had more experience than the others

46. Why couldn't the officials and satraps find anything to accuse Daniel of? (Daniel 6:4)

A. Daniel was a pastor
B. He was always kind to them
C. He was faithful and had no fault
D. He never talked to anyone

WEEK 4 MEMORY VERSE: PSALM 18:2
The LORD is my rock and my fortress and my deliverer; My God, my strength, in whom I will trust; My shield and the horn of my salvation, my stronghold.

47. How did the officials plan to trap Daniel? (Daniel 6:5-9)

A. They accused him of stealing

B. They made a law against prayer

C. They tricked the King into banning worship

D. Both B and C

48. What did Daniel do when he heard about the King's law? (Daniel 6:10)

A. He ran to the King to complain

B. He prayed at home like always

C. He secretly met with the officials

D. He stopped praying to avoid trouble

WEEK 4 MEMORY VERSE: PSALM 18:2

The LORD is my rock and my fortress and my deliverer; My God, my strength, in whom I will trust; My shield and the horn of my salvation, my stronghold.

49. What did King Darius do when Daniel was accused of not following the King's orders? (Daniel 6:12-17)

A. He ignored the accusation

B. He told the officials to arrest someone else

C. He let Daniel escape

D. He followed the law and had Daniel thrown in the den of lions, but hoped God would save him

50. What did the King say to Daniel before he was thrown into the lion's den? (Daniel 6:16)

A. Long live the King

B. May your God, whom you serve faithfully, save you

C. You will reap what you sow

D. I am so sorry

WEEK 4 MEMORY VERSE: PSALM 18:2

The LORD is my rock and my fortress and my deliverer; My God, my strength, in whom I will trust; My shield and the horn of my salvation, my stronghold.

WEEK 4

<<<<< WEEK 4 >>>>>

51. What happened after Daniel was thrown into the lion's den? (Daniel 6: 18-24)

A. The King couldn't sleep all night
B. The King rushed to check on Daniel the next morning
C. Daniel was alive, and his enemies were thrown into the den
D. All the above

52. How did God save Daniel from the lions? (Daniel 6:22)

A. Daniel fought off the lions
B. God sent an angel to shut their mouths
C. The lions were too full to eat
D. Daniel hid in a corner

WEEK 4 MEMORY VERSE: PSALM 18:2
The LORD is my rock and my fortress and my deliverer; My God, my strength, in whom I will trust; My shield and the horn of my salvation, my stronghold.

53. After God saved Daniel from the lions, what did King Darius declare? (Daniel 6: 26-27)

A. Everyone must respect the God of Daniel
B. God delivers and rescues
C. God does miracles in heaven and earth
D. All the above

54. What was said about the Son of Man in Daniel's vision? (Daniel 7:13-14)

A. He was given glory and a kingdom
B. His rule will never end
C. All nations will serve Him
D. All the above

WEEK 4 MEMORY VERSE: PSALM 18:2
The LORD is my rock and my fortress and my deliverer; My God, my strength, in whom I will trust; My shield and the horn of my salvation, my stronghold.

55. What did Angel Gabriel say about Daniel's vision? (Daniel 8:16-19)

A. It was about the end times
B. It showed the time of God's judgment
C. It was a warning for the past
D. Both A and B

56. Which book did Daniel read to understand the prophecy about Jerusalem? (Daniel 9:2)

A. Isaiah
B. Jeremiah
C. Nehemiah
D. Joshua

WEEK 4 MEMORY VERSE: PSALM 18:2
The LORD is my rock and my fortress and my deliverer; My God, my strength, in whom I will trust; My shield and the horn of my salvation, my stronghold.

Even when I go through fire, I will not be burned nor shall the flame scorch me – God is with me
(Isaiah 43:2)

Great job completing the week!

Did you memorize the daily verse?
Test yourself by writing it here...

_____

_____

_____

_____

_____

_____

Use this space to draw a scene from the Bible or reflect on something you learned, felt or experienced...

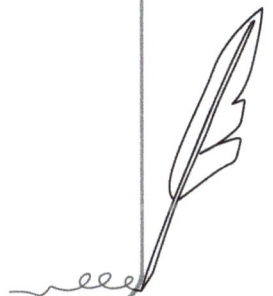

57. **What caused Daniel to pray and fast after reading the prophecy? (Daniel 9:2)**

A. He learned Jerusalem would be destroyed
B. He learned the people would suffer
C. He learned the city would be desolate for 70 years
D. He wanted a new vision

58. **What happened to the men who were with Daniel when he saw the vision by the river? (Daniel 10:7)**

A. They didn't see the vision
B. They became terrified
C. They ran and hid
D. All the above

WEEK 5 MEMORY VERSE: JAMES 1:12
Blessed is the man who endures temptation; for when he has been approved, he will receive the crown of life which the Lord has promised to those who love Him.

59. Why was Daniel's prayer delayed for 21 days? (Daniel 10:13)

A. Daniel sinned

B. The people were disobedient

C. A demonic prince blocked the angel

D. Daniel doubted God

60. Which angel helped deliver God's answer to Daniel? (Daniel 10:13)

A. Gabriel

B. Michael

C. Mishael

D. The angel of the Lord's presence

WEEK 5 MEMORY VERSE: JAMES 1:12

Blessed is the man who endures temptation; for when he has been approved, he will receive the crown of life which the Lord has promised to those who love Him.

61. Daniel was named Belteshazzar after the name of King Nebuchadnezzar's god (Daniel 4:8)

A. True

B. False

62. King Nebuchadnezzar was driven from among men so he could recognize God's authority. (Daniel 4:30-33)

A. True

B. False

WEEK 5 MEMORY VERSE: JAMES 1:12
Blessed is the man who endures temptation; for when he has been approved, he will receive the crown of life which the Lord has promised to those who love Him.

"

63. Daniel and his three friends were all thrown into the fiery furnace for refusing to bow to the golden image. (Daniel 3:12)

A. True
B. False

WEEK 5 MEMORY VERSE: JAMES 1:12

Blessed is the man who endures temptation; for when he has been approved, he will receive the crown of life which the Lord has promised to those who love Him.

INTRODUCTION: THE BOOK OF JOB

When Everything Falls Apart, God Still Holds You Together

The Book of **Job** is a raw and powerful story about **faith in suffering, trust through trials, and worship in the wilderness.** Job was a man who loved God and walked in righteousness — but he lost everything in a moment: his health, his wealth, and even his children.

Yet through all his pain, Job never cursed God. He cried, he questioned, he wrestled, but **he never let go**. And in the end, God not only restored him but revealed something even greater: **God is sovereign, faithful, and always near — even in silence.**

As you journey through Job, you will discover:
- **Suffering does not mean God has abandoned you**
- **Faith is proven when it's tested**
- **Worship is powerful, even when it hurts**
- **God's wisdom is far greater than ours**
- **God restores what was lost — and He gives double**

The Book of Job reminds us that we may not always understand what we're going through, but we can always trust the **God who sees it all.** When life feels unfair, God is still good. When questions are many, **He is still worthy**.

If you're ever walking through hard times, Job teaches you how to hold on to God with both hands, and come out stronger, wiser, and more blessed than before.

"Though He slay me, yet will I trust Him." — Job 13:15
"The Lord blessed the latter days of Job more than his beginning." — Job 42:12

64. Which of the following statements about Job is NOT true? (Job 1:1-3)

A. He was wealthy and the greatest of all the people of the East

B. He was blameless, upright, feared God, and shunned evil

C. He was a priest who led many offerings at the temple

D. He had many sons and daughters

65. What was Job's reason for offering burnt offerings for his children? (Job 1:4-5)

A. To purify them in case they had sinned

B. Because he feared they may have cursed God in their hearts

C. To seek God's continued favor for their lives

D. Because he was fulfilling his duty as a spiritual leader in the home

WEEK 5 MEMORY VERSE: JAMES 1:12

Blessed is the man who endures temptation; for when he has been approved, he will receive the crown of life which the Lord has promised to those who love Him.

66. What did God say concerning Job? (Job 1:8)

A. Job was God's servant
B. There was no one on earth like Job
C. Job was blameless, upright, feared God, and turned away from evil
D. All the above

**67. What did Satan say concerning Job?
(Job 1:9-11)**

A. Job only feared God because God had protected and blessed him
B. Job would curse God if everything was taken from him
C. Job was a great prophet of God
D. Both A and B

WEEK 5 MEMORY VERSE: JAMES 1:12
Blessed is the man who endures temptation; for when he has been approved, he will receive the crown of life which the Lord has promised to those who love Him.

68. God allowed Satan to test Job's faithfulness. What was Satan NOT allowed to touch? (Job 1:12)

A. His property
B. His children
C. His physical body
D. His wife

69. How did Job's children die? (Job 1:18-19)

A. There was a fire
B. They were poisoned
C. They died in their sleep
D. A house fell on them

WEEK 5 MEMORY VERSE: JAMES 1:12

Blessed is the man who endures temptation; for when he has been approved, he will receive the crown of life which the Lord has promised to those who love Him.

I am a crown of glory
and a royal diadem
in the hand of the LORD
(Isaiah 62:3)

Great job completing the week!

Did you memorize the daily verse?
Test yourself by writing it here...

_____

_____

_____

_____

_____

Use this space to draw a scene from the Bible or reflect
on something you learned, felt or experienced...

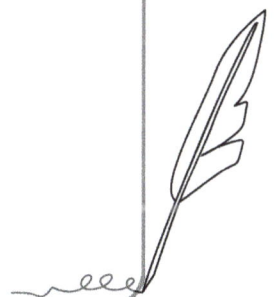

70. What did Job do when he lost everything he had? (Job 1:20-21)

A) He stood up, tore his robe, and shaved his head

B) He fell to the ground and worshipped God

C) He blessed the name of the Lord

D) All the above

71. When Satan presented himself before the Lord a second time, what did God say about Job? (Job 2:1–3)

A. Job was God's servant, and there was no one on earth like him

B. Job was blameless, upright, feared God, and turned away from evil

C. Job maintained his integrity even though he was harmed without cause

D. All the above

WEEK 6 MEMORY VERSE: JOB 13:15
Though He slay me, yet will I trust Him.
Even so, I will defend my own ways before Him.

72. What did Satan request permission to do to Job during the second test? (Job 2:4–5)

A. Kill his wife
B. Take away his anointing
C. Strike Job's health
D. Make him blind

73. What did Job do with the piece of broken pottery as he sat among the ashes? (Job 2:8)

A. He mended it to distract himself from the pain
B. He wanted to make another god with it
C. He scraped himself with it
D. He sat quietly and held it for comfort

WEEK 6 MEMORY VERSE: JOB 13:15
Though He slay me, yet will I trust Him.
Even so, I will defend my own ways before Him.

74. When Satan afflicted Job's body, what advice did Job's wife give him? (Job 2:9)

A. To call for a healer
B. To cry out to God for mercy
C. To curse God and die
D. To stay silent and endure

75. Which of the following was NOT Job's response to his wife's advice? (Job 2:10)

A. Job was grateful his wife was a virtuous woman
B. Job told his wife she was speaking like a foolish woman
C. Job asked if we should only accept good from God and not adversity
D. Job did not sin with his lips

WEEK 6 MEMORY VERSE: JOB 13:15
Though He slay me, yet will I trust Him.
Even so, I will defend my own ways before Him.

76. Which of the following was NOT one of Job's friends? (Job 2:11)

A. Ophir
B. Bildad
C. Zophar
D. Eliphaz

77. When Job's friends visited, why did they sit on the ground with him for seven days and nights? (Job 2:13)

A. They saw that Job's suffering was very great
B. Job was too sick to move
C. They prayed and fasted together
D. They did not want to leave him alone

WEEK 6 MEMORY VERSE: JOB 13:15
Though He slay me, yet will I trust Him.
Even so, I will defend my own ways before Him.

"

78. What did Eliphaz suggest was the reason for Job's suffering? (Job 4:1–8)

A. He was being punished because he had sinned

B. He was being punished because he was not prayerful

C. He was being punished because he was not a faithful giver

D. He was being punished because he was a proud man

"

79. What did Eliphaz suggest Job should do concerning his suffering? (Job 5:8)

A. Kill himself

B. Ask forgiveness from his friends

C. Seek God and present his case to Him

D. Fast and pray

WEEK 6 MEMORY VERSE: JOB 13:15
Though He slay me, yet will I trust Him.
Even so, I will defend my own ways before Him.

80. Who does great things too marvelous to understand and performs countless miracles? (Job 5:8–9)

A. God
B. Angels
C. Pastors
D. All the above

81. Happy is the man whom the Lord corrects. What should we not despise? (Job 5:17)

A. All men
B. Correction from the Lord
C. People who correct you
D. None of the above

WEEK 6 MEMORY VERSE: JOB 13:15
Though He slay me, yet will I trust Him.
Even so, I will defend my own ways before Him.

82. What did Job desire most from God in the midst of his suffering? (Job 6:8–10)

A. The restoration of his wealth

B. The forgiveness of his sins

C. The support of his friends

D. The release from his suffering through death

83. What does Job question God about concerning man? (Job 7:17–18)

A. Who is man that God has much regard for him

B. Who is man that God has set His heart on him

C. Who is man that God visits him every morning and tests him every moment

D. All the above

WEEK 6 MEMORY VERSE: JOB 13:15
Though He slay me, yet will I trust Him.
Even so, I will defend my own ways before Him.

I am strong in the Lord and in His mighty power
(Ephesians 6:10)

Great job completing the week!

**Did you memorize the daily verse?
Test yourself by writing it here...**

_____

_____

_____

_____

_____

_____

**Use this space to draw a scene from the Bible or reflect
on something you learned, felt or experienced...**

84. What conclusion did Bildad make concerning Job? (Job 8:3–5)

A. Job would be restored if he simply ignored his suffering

B. If Job prayed to God and was pure and did what was right, God would arise for him

C. God was unjust in allowing Job's trials

D. Job's suffering proved he was more righteous than others

85. What is the reason that Job did not question God? (Job 9:19, 32–33)

A. God is not a man

B. God is all righteous and strong

C. There is no one to mediate between God and Job

D. All the above

WEEK 7 MEMORY VERSE: JOB 19:25
I know that my redeemer lives, and that in the end
He will stand on the earth.

86. What did Job reflect on when pleading with God in his distress? (Job 10:8–12)

A. That God had formed him with His own hands
B. That God had clothed him with skin and bones
C. That God had granted him life and shown him favor
D. All the above

87. What did Zophar think of Job? (Job 11:1–6)

A. God was punishing Job far less than he deserved
B. Job deserved mercy
C. Job did not deserve what was happening to him
D. Job's family was destroyed because of Job

WEEK 7 MEMORY VERSE: JOB 19:25
I know that my redeemer lives, and that in the end
He will stand on the earth.

WEEK 7

88. What did Zophar recommend that Job should do in order for his life to get better?
(Job 11:13–17)

A. Prepare his heart and stretch out his hands toward God

B. Get rid of sins and iniquity

C. Not allow wickedness to dwell in his tents

D. All the above

89. What truth did Job declare about God's authority over all life? (Job 12:10)

A. In His hand is the life of every living thing

B. God shares His power with angels and kings

C. Man directs his own steps apart from God

D. Nature follows its own course without divine influence

WEEK 7 MEMORY VERSE: JOB 19:25
I know that my redeemer lives, and that in the end
He will stand on the earth.

WEEK 7

90. **What did Job say about his friends in response to their counsel? (Job 13:4–5)**

A. You are all worthless physicians
B. If only you would be silent, it would be your wisdom
C. You speak falsely on God's behalf
D. All the above

91. **What did Job say he would do even if God was to slay (kill) him? (Job 13:15)**

A. Put his trust in God
B. Remain silent
C. Defend God before others
D. Turn away from his faith

WEEK 7 MEMORY VERSE: JOB 19:25
I know that my redeemer lives, and that in the end
He will stand on the earth.

WEEK 7

92. Which of the following statements did Job make concerning life? (Job 14:1)

A. Man who is born of a woman is of few days and full of trouble

B. Life is always long and peaceful

C. Troubles only come to those who disobey

D. Life is full of joy for those who prosper

93. Why does Job say there is more hope for a tree than for a man? (Job 14:7–12)

A. If a tree is cut down, it can sprout again

B. Even if its root grows old, at the scent of water it will bud

C. But when a man dies, he does not rise

D. All the above

WEEK 7 MEMORY VERSE: JOB 19:25
I know that my redeemer lives, and that in the end
He will stand on the earth.

94. Job said, "All the days of my hard service I will _____." (Job 14:14)

A. Wait till my change comes
B. Praise the Lord
C. Be patient and wait on the Lord
D. Cry out for deliverance

95. How did Job describe his friends' attempts to comfort him? (Job 16:1–2)

A. They were like angels sent from God
B. They gave him peace and encouragement
C. They were miserable comforters
D. They prayed with him daily

WEEK 7 MEMORY VERSE: JOB 19:25
I know that my redeemer lives, and that in the end
He will stand on the earth.

WEEK 7

96. In his despair, how did Job describe his hope? (Job 17:11–15)

A. His hope would rise again like the morning sun

B. His hope had been uprooted and buried in the dust

C. His hope was in his Redeemer

D. His hope would come from his children

97. What confidence did Job express about God despite his suffering? (Job 19:25)

A. That God would vindicate him

B. That his Redeemer lives

C. That his enemies would fall

D. That he would regain all his wealth

WEEK 7 MEMORY VERSE: JOB 19:25
I know that my redeemer lives, and that in the end
He will stand on the earth.

My steps are ordered by the Lord, and He delights in my way

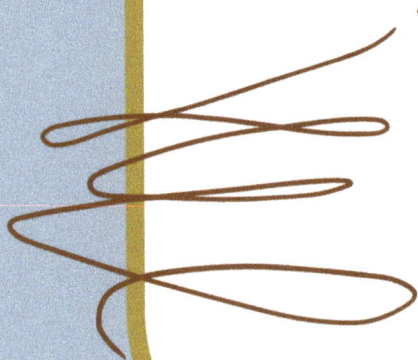

(Psalm 37:23)

Great job completing the week!

Did you memorize the daily verse?
Test yourself by writing it here...

_____

_____

_____

_____

_____

_____

Use this space to draw a scene from the Bible or reflect on something you learned, felt or experienced...

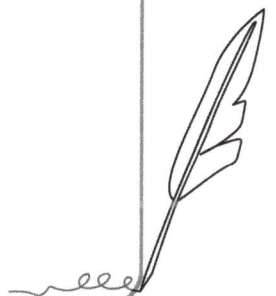

WEEK 8

98. After death, what was Job's greatest desire? (Job 19:25–27)

A. To see his family restored
B. To see his enemies punished
C. To see God with his own eyes
D. To live a long and peaceful life

99. What did Job observe about the lives of some wicked people? (Job 21:7-16)

A. They often live long, grow powerful, and die in peace
B. They are always destroyed quickly for their evil
C. They suffer more than the righteous in this life
D. They never experience joy or prosperity

WEEK 8 MEMORY VERSE: JEREMIAH 32:27

I am the LORD, the God of all mankind. Is anything too hard for me?

100. What did Job say about the success of the wicked? (Job 24:13-24)

A. They enjoy prosperity for a time, then are cut off
B. They always suffer for their wrongdoing
C. Their children are cursed with sorrow
D. They never experience good things

101. How does Job describe the power and majesty of God? (Job 26:14)

A. God's power is limited
B. God's power and majesty are beyond human understanding
C. God's power is comparable to human rulers
D. Job did not speak of God's power and majesty

WEEK 8 MEMORY VERSE: JEREMIAH 32:27
I am the LORD, the God of all mankind. Is anything too hard for me?

WEEK 8

102. **According to Job, what is wisdom?**
(Job 28:28)

A. Knowledge
B. Truth
C. God
D. The fear of the Lord

103. **According to Job, what is understanding?**
(Job 28:28)

A. Turning away from evil
B. Knowledge
C. Truth
D. Fear of the Lord

WEEK 8 MEMORY VERSE: JEREMIAH 32:27
I am the LORD, the God of all mankind. Is anything too hard for me?

WEEK 8

104. According to Job, what was the reason behind the blessings and success he once had? (Job 29:2-11)

A. His own wisdom and intelligence

B. Luck and chance

C. The hand of God was upon him

D. The support of friends and family

105. According to Job, how did people respond to him in his former days? (Job 29:21-25)

A. They mocked him, even though they once respected him

B. They admired and respected him

C. They pitied and consoled him

D. They ignored and disregarded him

WEEK 8 MEMORY VERSE: JEREMIAH 32:27

I am the LORD, the God of all mankind. Is anything too hard for me?

106. How did Job describe those who mocked him in his suffering? (Job 30:1-8)

A. They were once outcasts he would not have hired
B. They were noble leaders who turned on him
C. They were his family and closest friends
D. They were wise and honored men of the city

107. How did Job describe his current state compared to his past? (Job 30:16-19)

A. He is blessed and prosperous
B. He is content and at peace
C. He is experiencing deep sorrow and affliction
D. None of the above

WEEK 8 MEMORY VERSE: JEREMIAH 32:27
I am the LORD, the God of all mankind. Is anything too hard for me?

WEEK 8

108. What did Job say about God's response to his cries for help? (Job 30:20–23)

A. God answered and rescued him

B. God delivered him speedily

C. God ignored him

D. Both A and B are correct

109. According to Job, what is the consequence of committing adultery? (Job 31:9-12)

A. It is a sin deserving of judgment

B. It leads to financial ruin

C. It brings public shame but not spiritual consequence

D. It is acceptable if no one is hurt

WEEK 8

110. **Which of the following did Job consider to be a sin, deserving of judgment?**
(Job 31:24-28)

A. Trusting in wealth
B. Worshiping the sun or moon
C. Denying God
D. All the above

111. **Why did Elihu say he had remained silent while Job and his friends spoke?**
(Job 32:4–7)

A. Because he was afraid of offending Job
B. Because his friends were older, and he thought age brought wisdom
C. Because he didn't understand the situation
D. Because God told him not to speak

WEEK 8 MEMORY VERSE: JEREMIAH 32:27
I am the LORD, the God of all mankind. Is anything too hard for me?

The Lord is fighting for me,
I need only to be still
(Exodus 14:14)

Great job completing the week!

Did you memorize the daily verse?
Test yourself by writing it here...

_____

_____

_____

_____

_____

_____

Use this space to draw a scene from the Bible or reflect on something you learned, felt or experienced...

WEEK 9

112. **According to Elihu, how does God often speak to mankind? (Job 33:14-18)**

A. Through dreams and visions
B. Through thunder and earthquakes
C. Through prophets alone
D. God no longer speaks to people

113. **How did Elihu describe Job's attitude toward God's dealings with him? (Job 34:35-37)**

A. Job was humble and repentant
B. Job was ignorant and rebellious
C. Job was silent and submissive
D. Job was righteous and understanding

WEEK 9 MEMORY VERSE: JOB 42:2

I know that You can do everything, and that no purpose of Yours can be withheld from You.

WEEK 9

114. **How did Elihu describe God's control over the weather?** (Job 37:6–13)

A. God does not control the weather
B. God favors certain regions with good weather
C. God is in complete control and directs all aspects of the weather
D. Elihu did not talk about the weather at all

115. **How should people respond to God's power and greatness?** (Job 37:23–24)

A. Ignore His presence and rely on their own strength
B. Fear God and show reverence
C. Question His ways and seek personal understanding
D. Pray only when facing hardship

WEEK 9 MEMORY VERSE: JOB 42:2

I know that You can do everything, and that no purpose of Yours can be withheld from You.

WEEK 9

116. What did God ask Job about the foundations of the earth? (Job 38:4–6)

A. Where he was when God laid them
B. If he understood how the earth was supported
C. Both A and B
D. None of the above

**117. Which animal did God say treats her young as though they are not hers?
(Job 39:13–18)**

A. Lion
B. Eagle
C. Goat
D. Ostrich

WEEK 9 MEMORY VERSE: JOB 42:2

I know that You can do everything, and that no purpose of Yours can be withheld from You.

118. Which animal did God describe as mocking fear and having a powerful, snorting strength? (Job 39:19–25)

A. Lion

B. Horse

C. Ox

D. Goat

119. What was the purpose of God's questions to Job in Chapter 40? (Job 40:6–14)

A. To reveal His power and wisdom to Job

B. To mock Job for complaining

C. To confuse Job with difficult questions

D. To punish Job for doubting

WEEK 9 MEMORY VERSE: JOB 42:2

I know that You can do everything, and that no purpose of Yours can be withheld from You.

120. In Job Chapter 41, which fearsome creature does God describe in great detail?
(Job 41:1–10)

A. Leviathan

B. Behemoth

C. Dragon

D. Serpent

121. What does God say about anyone trying to capture Leviathan? (Job 41:1–10)

A. Any hope of overcoming Leviathan is false

B. No one is fierce enough to stir Leviathan up

C. Leviathan would submit to the brave

D. Both A and B

WEEK 9 MEMORY VERSE: JOB 42:2
I know that You can do everything, and that no purpose of Yours can be withheld from You.

122. What is the main message behind God's description of Leviathan? (Job 41:1–11)

A. God's warning against sea monsters
B. God's emphasis on His power and dominion over all creation
C. A lesson in marine biology
D. That creatures will always obey man

123. How did Job respond after hearing God's questions and speeches? (Job 42:1–6)

A. He sat in dust and ashes to show repentance
B. He confessed he had spoken of things too wonderful for him
C. He said he had only heard of God before, but now he saw Him
D. All the above

WEEK 9 MEMORY VERSE: JOB 42:2

I know that You can do everything, and that no purpose of Yours can be withheld from You.

WEEK 9

124. Why was God angry at Eliphaz and his two friends? (Job 42:7)

A. Because they did not take good care of Job
B. Because they caused Job to doubt God
C. Because they had not spoken rightly about God, as Job had
D. Because they did not offer sacrifices

125. What did God command Eliphaz and his two friends to do to make things right with Him? (Job 42:8)

A. Offer seven bulls and seven rams as a burnt offering
B. Ask Job to pray for them
C. Fast and pray for seven days
D. Both A and B

WEEK 9 MEMORY VERSE: JOB 42:2
I know that You can do everything, and that no purpose of Yours can be withheld from You.

BONUS QUESTIONS

126. What happened after Job prayed for his friends? (Job 42:10-12)

A. The Lord restored Job's fortunes and gave him twice as much
 B. His family returned with gifts of silver and gold
 C. Job's latter days were more blessed than his beginning
 D. All the above

127. Which of the following was NOT one of Job's daughters? (Job 42:14)

A. Karen-Happuch
B. Keturah
C. Keziah
D. Jemimah

WEEK 9 MEMORY VERSE: JOB 42:2
I know that You can do everything, and that no purpose of Yours can be withheld from You.

The Lord shall perfect all that concerns me (Psalm 138:8)

Great job completing the week!

Did you memorize the daily verse?
Test yourself by writing it here...

_____

_____

_____

_____

_____

Use this space to draw a scene from the Bible or reflect on something you learned, felt or experienced...

Certificate of Completion

This Certificate Certifies That:

_____

Has Successfully Completed The Daniel & Job Workbook!

Flo & Grace

_____   _____

PARENT/TEACHER SIGNATURE   **PROJECT KINGDOM COME**

WOULD YOU LIKE TO ACCEPT JESUS INTO YOUR HEART?

THE BIBLE SAYS:

If you confess with your mouth that Jesus is Lord and believe in your heart that God has raised Him from the dead, you will be saved
(Romans 10:9)

SAY THE PRAYER BELOW OUT LOUD AND BELIEVE IT IN YOUR HEART!

Dear Lord Jesus,
I know that I am a sinner, and I ask for Your forgiveness.
I believe You died for my sins and rose from the dead.
I repent of my sins and invite You to come into my heart and life.
I want to trust and follow You as my Lord and Savior. Help me to live for you for the rest of my life.
I am now a child of God, and I ask You to fill me with Your Holy Spirit.

In Jesus' Name I pray, Amen.

Congratulations!
If you have prayed this prayer, please let an adult know or send an email to mybibleworkbooks@gmail.com

<<<<<< ANSWER KEY: >>>>>>

1. B
2. A
3. B
4. B
5. A
6. A
7. A
8. A
9. C
10. C
11. B
12. B

13. D
14. A
15. D
16. D
17. C
18. B
19. B
20. D
21. D
22. A
23. C
24. D

25. D
26. C
27. A
28. B
29. A
30. D
31. D
32. B
33. D
34. D
35. A
36. D

ANSWER KEY:

37. D	49. D	61. A
38. D	50. B	62. A
39. D	51. D	63. B
40. D	52. B	64. C
41. A	53. D	65. B
42. B	54. D	66. D
43. D	55. D	67. D
44. B	56. B	68. C
45. C	57. C	69. D
46. C	58. D	70. D
47. D	59. C	71. D
48. B	60. B	72. C

73. C	85. D	97. B
74. C	86. D	98. C
75. A	87. A	99. A
76. A	88. D	100. A
77. A	89. A	101. B
78. A	90. D	102. D
79. C	91. A	103. A
80. A	92. A	104. C
81. B	93. D	105. B
82. D	94. A	106. A
83. D	95. C	107. C
84. D	96. B	108. C

ANSWER KEY:

109. A
110. D
111. B
112. A
113. B
114. C
115. B
116. C
117. D
118. B
119. A
120. A

121. D
122. B
123. D
124. C
125. D
126. D
127. B

PLEASE GIVE US YOUR FEEDBACK!

Please send us your feedback on this workbook. We would love to hear what you enjoyed most, and ways you think it could be improved!

Please Send an email to: MyBibleWorkbooks@gmail.com, or leave us a comment on one of our social media pages.

MyBibleWorkbooks@gmail.com

Projectkingdomcome

Projectkingdomcome

SCAN ME

> "And I am certain that God, who began the good work within you, will continue His work until it is finally finished on the day when Christ Jesus returns.

Philippians 1:6

DRAW HERE

DRAW HERE

DRAW HERE

DRAW HERE

9 781961 786165